On Fire Leadership™

Motivational Quotes for
Martial Artists

DAVE GERBER

Special Contribution by
Bob Zacharias
7th Dan Black Belt, Tae Kwon Do

Timeless Publishing

www.onfireleadershipquotes.com

ISBN 978-0-9788707-6-8

Timeless Publishing
www.timelesspublishing.com
info@timelesspublishing.com

Design by Gaye Newton
Author photograph by Robert Merhaut
Special Contributor Photo by D-T and Me Photography
Cover images by Thinkstock

Printed in the United States of America

Testimonials from Martial Artists

"As a martial artist with several different backgrounds and a professional fighter/coach, I can truly appreciate the time and energy Dave has put into creating this gift for the MA community. I absolutely will use this on a daily basis, in support of my gym, team and self. Great read, no matter what page I start on. Thanks Dave!"

~ Marcus Kowal, 2nd Dan Black Belt Krav Maga
    Systems Gym Head Coach and Gym Owner

"On Fire Leadership is a great example of what Dave Gerber does. A leader must provide purpose and motivation. No one understands that more than Dave, and no one inspires more than he does. To motivate yourself means to search for inspiration that speaks into your soul. With this book, you can pick from inspirational quotes from different disciplines and even different eras of time. When it comes to motivational leadership, these handpicked quotes have something for everyone. Nice job, Dave!"

~ Dennis Fivecoat, Martial Arts Instructor
    Multiple black belts, multiple disciplines
    US Army (Retired)

"Everybody knows the power of a good quote when leading or looking for a little extra energy. Here are 180 great ones!"

~ Melanie Smith, Martial Artist, multiple disciplines
    Black Belt, Martial Arts Instructor

"To truly defend yourself, you need to find what I like to call 'THAT INNER HULK' from within. It's the ability to become instantaneously aggressive, when self-preservation depends on it. This book taps into it!"

~ Troy Osgood, Martial Arts Instructor, multiple disciplines
Fire Investigator

"I love this book, every martial artist can find powerful words to enhance their training and their life."

~ Juanita Howanic, Martial Arts Instructor
Multiple Disciplines

"Great motivational book, going right in my gym bag next to all the essentials!"

~ Hank Swann, Martial Artist, multiple disciplines
Executive and Personal Trainer

"You are never out of the fight, whether it is in life or on your personal journey. This book is a great reminder!"

~ Dennis Cappo, Martial Artist, multiple disciplines
Business Owner

"Dave Gerber's outstanding collection of quotes inspires and reminds us of the characteristics leaders and martial artists should embody. Truly motivational!"

~ Brandon Ferguson, Multiple Black Belts, Lead Instructor

Dedication

From Dave Gerber

To the spirit and energy of Bruce Lee, the man, father, philosopher, Martial Artist, actor and bridge between the eastern and western hemispheres. His energy has translated into so much motivation and inspiration…for me and so many generations of people in so many countries. Amazing! It is my hope that people get to see all sides of Master Lee, for that is truly what made this man a legend.

I also want to dedicate this to all of those individuals who have been helpful, fun, supportive, caring and truly professional when helping me develop my skills. I will forever be hungry and humble, a student of anyone who wants to teach me.

From Bob Zacharias

This book is dedicated to all those who mentored me in my youth. From my coaches, teachers, other martial artists that I trained with to my neighbors who guided me along the way. Thank you for taking the time with me and others. I have been following your example and carrying the torch over the last 35 years.

Also by Dave Gerber

On Fire Leadership: A Leader's Book of Motional Quotes

On Fire Leadership: Motivational Quotes for Military Leaders

On Fire Leadership: Motivational Quotes for Educators

S.A.F.E. Self-Defense™: For Kids From a Kid!

S.A.F.E. Self-Defense™: For Kids From a Kid! (Ground Techniques and More!)

S.A.F.E. Self-Defense™: Graduation, College Bound and Beyond!

Turn $oft $kills into Hard Money: A Leader's Conflict Calculator

Conquering Project Management Conflict

Use Conflict: Advance Your Winning Life

Don't Learn the Hard Way! Pre-Marriage Questions So You Don't Get Divorced (Again)

www.DaveGerber.com

www.Synergydt.com

www.Synergy-Selfdefense.com

For more information about this book and others:

www.onfireleadershipquotes.com

Foreword
By George Buruian.

5th Dan Black Belt in TAEKWONDO
3rd Dan Black Belt in Alpha Krav Maga
Former Romanian Olympic TAEKWONDO Coach
Martial Arts Masters Hall of Fame

They say that a life of martial arts is a marathon, not a sprint. Reality, it is both. You had better know when to coast, when to sprint, when to run and when to find a solid pace, sometimes all in the same day or encounter. From my early beginnings through a 35 year continuing journey, I know that my marathon continues.

Acknowledgement from others has never been on my list to do or achieve. In approaching my life this way, I believe I have been better able to make an impact on others' lives in a positive way, both athletes at all levels and the people I engage with who do not practice any martial arts.

My core values have been solidified over the course of my role as a martial arts coach, whether in the gym, working with Olympic athletes, and as a practitioner myself. Over the course of many years, my knowledge from distinct styles has grown, and I now draw upon several for my own training, not to mention the increased fun and motivation.

Inspiring others to achieve and go beyond their limitations has been a mainstay for me over the last several decades. In my earlier days, I was focused on developing myself as a Martial Artist. Now I devote my time, passion and energy to others so that each may go further than they ever thought they could.

With this collection of motivational quotes, Dave Gerber has chosen to give back to the MA community at large. It is a great read that will keep you turning the pages, looking for more insights from many of the greatest the world has ever seen. As a professional motivator, it is clear that Dave worked to bridge the gap between the different disciples and provide both teachers and students great, famous words to live by.

One becomes a beginner after one thousand days of training and an expert after ten thousand days of practice.

~Mas Oyama

The leg of a baby is stronger than
the balls of Mohamed Ali.
~Imi Lichtenfeld

The key to immortality is first
living a life worth remembering.
~Bruce Lee

Introduction
By Bob Zacharias, 7th Dan Black Belt, Tae Kwon Do

"A true champion is one who sweats from exhaustion when no one is watching."

~Bas Rutten

Throughout my life, and with my Martial Arts experiences for the last thirty years, I have found that sometimes people's lives can be changed with only a few words.

The Bas quote above, for example, does just that. He reminds me that throughout my entire Martial Arts career, I have been supported by the best people with great intentions, and yet I have also spent much time in the gym alone.

Not lonely; that would imply that I have gone to the gym each day, each night without purpose. No, when I am alone, working hard, no one watching, that is when I know I have deepened my level of care for myself and my training. I usually leave the gym, on those and most occasions, with a gentle smile of accomplishment. I am not training for a fight, I am training for life.

The use of powerful quotes has always been a part of my work and approach, not to mention when other instructors or professional speakers use them, the words usually resonate with me as a call to action.

This book is just that, a call to action—a call to pick up the action or intensity or motivation or desire to reach out and try to inspire someone new to start.

Being a part of this project hopefully extends my reach into the lives of martial artists everywhere, both practitioners and instructors. It is very exciting to work with

Dave, and I am honored we have the opportunity to collaborate.

This book, Dave Gerber's creation, represents a burning desire to give something tangible back to the martial arts community. Something that can be a source of inspiration for those around the world, regardless of their discipline, is extremely admirable. The prolific approach towards giving back to the larger community, both with this book and his others, is in itself, inspiring for me. Those who know him are impressed by his unyielding desire to bring forth positive social change while speaking to people. He provides contagious passion and increased motivation, instantly.

We hope you enjoy these quotes and keep them handy, whether you are a coach, practitioner or both!

1

If you love life, don't waste time,
for time is what life is made up of.
 ~ Bruce Lee

2

A warrior's strength is in the size
of his heart. He shows love, honor,
and respect. He will stand and
fight in the face of adversity for
the ones he loves. He will be their
voice. He will be their shield. He
leads by example, always
remembering who he is.

 ~ Sam Sade

3

Learning jiu-jitsu is something for the subconscious, not for the consciousness.

~ Helio Gracie

4

Discipline and consistency. I owe these two factors all have attained in my life. Things have never happened overnight. Results have appeared as a consequence of decade's long toil. It is necessary to persist.

~ Carlos Gracie Jr.

5

No one will hit you harder than life itself. It doesn't matter how hard you hit back. It's about how much you can take, and keep fighting, how much you can suffer and keep moving forward. That's how you win.
 ~ Anderson Silva

6

A true warrior is always armed with three things—the radiant sword of pacification; the mirror of bravery, wisdom and friendship; and the precious jewel of enlightenment.
 ~ Morihei Ueshiba

7

My attitude is I train like a
champion, win like a champion,
and if I lose, I lose like a
champion.
  ~ Cung Le

8

I like this feeling of weariness after
training, when I'm walking home
exhausted, dragging my feet. I like
this a lot.
  ~ Fedor Emelianenko

9

When I was in school, martial arts made you a dork, and I became self-conscious that I was too masculine. I was a 16-year-old girl with ringworm and cauliflower ears. People made fun of my arms and called me "Miss Man." It wasn't until I got older that I realized: These people are idiots. I'm fabulous.

~ Ronda Rousey

10

I just want to be known as the best ever. Is that too much to ask?
~ BJ Penn

11

Seek not to follow in the footsteps
of men of old; seek what they
sought.
~ Matsu Basho

12

For me, the martial arts is a search
for something inside. It's not just a
physical discipline.
 ~ Brandon Lee

13

There is a difference between a
fighter and a martial artist. A
fighter is training for a purpose:
He has a fight. I'm a martial artist.
I don't train for a fight. I train for
myself. I'm training all the time.
My goal is perfection. But I will
never reach perfection.

~ Georges St-Pierre

14

A lot of people give up just before
they're about to make it. You know
you never know when that next
obstacle is going to be the last one.

~ Chuck Norris

15

Nothing is more harmful to the world than a martial art that is not effective in actual self-defense.
~ Choki Motobu

16

The perfect technique is one without much effort or conscious thought applied at the right time in the right direction, with the right amount of force – a spontaneous reaction to the opportunity presented by the opponent's movement.
~ Unknown

17

It's all about having confidence in
yourself. I don't fear that man
standing across from me.
~ Ken Shamrock

18

Spirit first, technique second.
~ Gichin Funakoshi

19

If you don't give up, eventually
you will break the cycle, and you
will overcome any obstacle.
 ~ Lyoto Machida

20

The ultimate aim of Karate lies not
in victory or defeat but in the
perfection of character of the
participants.

 ~ Gichin Funakoshi

21

Do not let circumstances control you. You change your circumstances.

~ Jackie Chan

22

Everything inspires me. This fight, my career, my life, my daughter, my family my team, are my inspiration. My fans are my inspiration. Everything inspires me, and I take whatever I can as inspiration.

~ Mauricio "Shogun" Rua

23

What you practice is what you
will do.
 ~ Benny Urquidez

24

If you want to be a lion, you must
train with lions.
 ~ Carlson Gracie

25

It is difficult for a student to pick a good teacher, but it is more difficult for a teacher to pick a good student.

~ Grandmaster Ip Man

26

Every tomorrow has two handles. We can take hold of it by the handle of anxiety, or by the handle of faith.

~ Author Unknown

27

One must try every day to expand one's limits.

~ Mas Oyama

28

A punch should stay like a treasure in the sleeve. It should not be used indiscriminately.

~ Chotoku Kyan

29

I fear not the man who has
practiced 10,000 kicks once, but I
fear the man who has practiced
one kick 10,000 times.
 ~ Bruce Lee

30

What matters most is continuation
and imagination, which lead to
power.
 ~ Kazushi Sakuraba

31

Should you desire the great tranquility, prepare to sweat.

~ Hakuin

32

If I am going to leave something behind, if I am going to leave a message, or a lifestyle, it's to never surrender in the face of adversity. Even in the fight you have to go a little further, a little more, a little more, a little more. In the "little more" you will last much longer than you thought you could. Believe in your dreams, and work hard for them.

~ Wanderlei Silva

33

Every time you lose, it's good
because you see something is
amiss. The guy who's on top with
no effort just settles.
~ Antonio Rodrigo Nogueira

34

Be motivated…don't be a
thermometer, be a thermostat. Set
your own temperature. You can
do whatever you want, just make
sure it is good and right. Put your
mind into it, you can do it.
~ Vitor Belfort

35

It is important that karate can be practiced by the young and old, men and women alike. That is, since there is no need for a special training place, equipment, or an opponent. A flexibility in training is provided such that the physically and spiritually weak individual can develop his body and mind so gradually and naturally that he himself may not even realize his own great progress.

~ Funakoshi Gichin

36

I believe the world is one big family, and we need to help each other.

~ Jet Li

37

In the fight, only one person can be comfortable. Your job is to transfer the comfortable from your opponent to you.
~ Rickson Gracie

38

Martial art is a form of expression—an expression from your inner self to your hands and legs.
~ Donnie Yen

39

I practice martial arts not to win
over other people but to win over
my own heart.
 ~ Tony Jaa

40

Your body is like a piece of
dynamite. You can tap it with a
pencil all day, but you'll never
make it explode. You hit it once
with a hammer: Bang! Get serious.
Do 40 hard minutes, not an hour
and half of nonsense. It's so much
more rewarding.
 ~ Jason Statham

41

No matter how you excel in the art of "Ti" (Okinawan precursor to Karate) and in your scholastic endeavors, nothing is more important than your behavior and humanity as observed in daily life.

~ Junsoku Uekata

42

If you know the enemy and know yourself you need not fear the results of a hundred battles.

~ Sun Tzu

43

One of the most important things
any beginner needs to learn is how
to expose the structure of a tree.
Until we do this, our plants are
just bushes.
  ~ Masahiko Kimura

44

Judo teaches us to look for the best
possible course of action, whatever the individual circumstances,
and helps us to understand that
worry is a waste of energy.
  ~ Jigoro Kano

45

We learn martial arts as helping weakness. You never fight for people to get hurt. You're always helping people.
 ~ Jackie Chan

46

Why waltz with a guy for 10 rounds if you can knock him out in one?

 ~ Rocky Marciano

47

We distract, we destroy, we go
home.
~Sam Sade

48

All the champions—you go and
ask Mike Tyson or Joe Louis,
Rocky Marciano, Lennox Lewis
and myself included. And I'm
sorry for putting myself in line
with all the other great names, but
the champion's attitude is it
doesn't matter who is in front of
me, I am going to conquer this
person and win the fight and
knock the person out.

~ Wladimir Klitschko

49

The ultimate aim of martial arts is
not having to use them.
  ~ Miyamoto Musashi

50

When I was growing up, there
were times I had to compete
against boys in Tae Kwon Do, and
I'd show them right away that I
wasn't someone to mess with.
  ~ Katheryn Winnick

51

The best way to get a move to
work is to make it so uncom-
fortable that the opponent gives it
to you to stop the pain.
~ Carlson Gracie

52

If you spend too much time
thinking about a thing, you'll
never get it done.
~ Bruce Lee

53

You know what the true definition of hell is? It's when you die, you get to meet the person you could have been.

~ Anonymous

54

Nothing under the sun is greater than education. By educating one person and sending him into the society of his generation, we make a contribution extending a hundred generations to come.

~ Kano Jigoro

55

The losses in the cage, yeah they
hurt, but they're nothing like the
wins that I've received.
  ~ Jens Pulver

56

You're standing in the cage and
you've got two options—you can
quit or you can continue going,
and I'm not a quitter.
  ~ Rich Franklin

57

All my life, following the warrior's code has taken me to places that I was afraid to go. But when I got there I was glad I made the journey.
  ~ Frank Shamrock

58

The obstacle is the path.
  ~ Zen Proverb

59

Curiosity is what kills fear.
  ~ Greg Jackson

60

To all those whose progress
remains hampered by ego-related
distractions, let humility—the
spiritual cornerstone upon which
Karate rests—serve to remind one
to place virtue before vice, values
before vanity and principles
before personalities.
  ~ Sokon "Bushi" Matsumura

61

The purpose of training is to
tighten up the slack, toughen the
body, and polish the spirit.
  ~ Morihei Ueshiba

62

How you train is how it will come
out.
  ~ David James

63

I practice the martial arts. I don't practice MMA. MMA is my job, MMA is a new sport. Martial arts is the knowledge from the ages.

~ Anderson Silva

64

I see martial arts as moving forms of meditation. When you're sparring or drilling techniques, you can't think of anything else.

~ Joe Rogan

65

I love martial arts. I'm obsessed
with it. Martial arts is my baby.
It's not my moneymaker. It's my
all. It's my world. It's my
enthusiasm.

~ Jon Jones

66

To me, the extraordinary aspect of
martial arts lies in its simplicity.
The easy way is also the right way,
and martial arts is nothing at all
special; the closer to the true way
of martial arts, the less wastage of
expression there is.

~ Bruce Lee

67

If you know the art of breathing,
you have the strength, wisdom
and courage of ten tigers.
  ~ Chinese adage

68

Just to succeed in life, whatever it
may be, as a mixed martial artist,
father, husband, that's what
inspires me.
  ~ Frankie Edgar

69

I think the key is never being satisfied with your skills, and you have to constantly learn. I say this all the time. I sound like a broken record, but if you are not getting better in this sport you are getting worse.

~ Kenny Florian

70

What you put into it is what you're going to get out of it. This thing is so big now, if you're getting the chance to step into the octagon, you better be going full speed and give it everything you've got.

~ BJ Penn

71

We all have inner demons to fight. We call these demons "fear" and "hatred" and "anger." If you don't conquer them, then a life of a hundred years... is a tragedy. If you do, a life of a single day can be a triumph.

~ Yip Man

72

There is no finish line. When you reach one goal, find a new one.

~ Chuck Norris

73

I am a student of whoever I can learn from.

~ Rashad Evans

74

Empty your mind. Be formless, shapeless like water. If you put water into a cup, it becomes the cup. If you put water into a bottle, it becomes the bottle. You put it into a teapot, it becomes the teapot. Now, water can flow or it can crash. Be water, my friend.

~ Bruce Lee

75

Even the most powerful human being has a limited sphere of strength. Draw him outside of that sphere and into your own, and his strength will dissipate.

~ Morihei Ueshiba

76

Beginnings are easy. The key is to finish the race.

~ Vitor Belfort

77

He that is taught only by himself
has a fool for a master.

~ Ben Jonson

78

A warrior may choose pacifism;
others are condemned to it.

~ Author unknown

79

Two Zen monks were walking along a river when they came upon a beautiful young woman. The bridge was out, she tearfully explained, and she needed to cross the river right away. "Don't worry," said one of the monks, "just climb on my back and I'll carry you across." The girl climbed on the monk's back and he took her across. The monks then continued on their journey, but the second monk was very upset. Finally he couldn't stand it anymore and said, "How could you, a virtuous monk, allow an attractive young lady to ride upon your back?" The first monk said, "Are you still carrying that lady? I put her down when we crossed the river."

~ Zen Buddhist story

80

One of the quotes that I use a lot—
besides you're only as good as the
guys you sweat and bleed with—is
that iron sharpens iron. So that one
man sharpens another. I think that
it is very true. If you are not in a
training environment where you
are getting smacked in the head,
you are getting tapped out, you are
getting challenged on a daily basis,
then you are not getting any better.
You're not improving. Your
workout partners are a very
important piece of your progression
as an athlete and the character that
you are building as a person as
well. Those are key components
and finding that right place is a
piece of it.

~ Randy Couture, *Wrestling For
   Fighting*

81

Focus on the positive, that's what I
tell my kids, and everything will
take care of itself.
 ~ Dan Henderson

82

Karate aims to build character,
improve human behavior, and
cultivate modesty; it does not,
however, guarantee it.
 ~ Yasuhiro Konishi

83

To see a man beaten not by a
better opponent but by himself is a
tragedy.
 ~ Cus D'Amato

84

You can beat me up, but don't
touch my hair. I will kill you!
 ~ Jet Li

85

Being an artist is something much bigger than just a fight.

~ Greg Jackson

86

Mental strength is really important because you either win or lose in your mind. And I'm not solely talking about sport matches, boxing events. Anything you do, you at first start with your mental strength. And you can actually train and develop it, and I am responsible for what I'm saying because I have experience with that.

~ Wladimir Klitschko

87

If you do not know others and do not know yourself, you will be in danger in every single battle.
~ Sun Tzu

88

When your temper rises, lower your fists. When your fists rise, lower your temper.
~ Chojun Miyagi

89

To win one hundred victories in one hundred battles is not the highest skill. To subdue the enemy without fighting is the highest skill.
  ~ Gichin Funakoshi

90

Why did I become Jackie Chan? Mostly because I work very hard. When people were sleeping, I was still training.
  ~ Jackie Chan

91

The most important thing that I've figured out is that things work out the way they're supposed to. We try to have all this control and fashion things the way we want, but everything happens for a reason, and in the end it works out the way it's supposed to.

~ Randy Couture

92

Martial arts is not about fighting; it's about building character.

~ Bo Bennett

93

If you think, you are late. If you
are late, you use strength. If you
use strength, you tire. And if you
tire, you die.

~ Saulo Ribeiro

94

I definitely feel I do have God in
my corner.

~ Chuck Norris

95

One of the greatest gifts of martial
arts is that they ultimately guide
us to new levels of spirituality.
~ Joseph Cardillo

96

Fear is conquered by action.
When we challenge our fears, we
defeat them. When we grapple
with our difficulties, they lose
their hold upon us. When we dare
to face the things which scare us,
we open the door to freedom.
~ Author Unknown

97

And the day came when the risk
to remain tight in a bud became
more painful than the risk it took
to blossom.

~ Anais Nin

98

If you don't design your own life
plan, chances are you'll fall into
someone else's plan. And guess
what they have planned for you?
Not much.

~ Jim Rohn

99

That which does not kill us, must have missed us.

~ Miowara Tomokata

100

Karate is not about winning. It's about not losing.

~ Shigetoshi Senaha

101

Cowards die many times before their deaths; the valiant never taste death but once.

~ William Shakespeare, *Julius Caesar*

102

Motivation is what gets you started. Habit is what keeps you going.

~ Jim Ryun

103

Real living is living for others.
~ Bruce Lee

104

Do not try to fight a lion if you are
not one yourself.
~ African Proverb

105

When you are content to be
simply yourself and don't
compare or compete, everybody
will respect you.
 ~ Lao-Tzu

106

I do not talk about my
weaknesses, I work on them.

 ~ Fedor Emelianenko

107

When someone is fearless, when pain isn't a factor, it's impossible to break his spirit. And a fighter with heart will almost always win out against a fighter with skill but no will.

~ Chuck Lidell

108

If you don't believe in yourself than you have no business pursuing a title or something like that, you don't have any business in pursuit of being the best.

~ Rich Franklin

109

Natural movement is the shortest way to an effective result. Like the way the water runs, it always finds the right way.

~ Vladimir Vasiliev

110

Knowing is not enough. We must apply. Willing is not enough: we must do.

~ Bruce Lee

111

It's not the dog in the fight, but the fight in the dog that counts.

~ Mark Twain

112

Those who cannot bravely face danger are the slaves of their attackers.

~ Aristotle

113

The greatest power is often simple patience.

~ E. Joseph Cossman

114

I'm actually listening to my body now. My body needs freedom. When I train I create serenity and I produce oxygen in my blood. It helps me to think better and relax.

~ Jean-Claude Van Damme

115

It is better to do too much than to do too little.

~ Bas Rutten

116

You walk into a room and you want people to know your presence, without you doing anything.

~ Wesley Snipes

117

In the old days, we trained Karate as a martial art, but now they train Karate as a gymnastic sport. I think we must avoid treating Karate as a sport—it must be a martial art at all times! Your fingers and the tips of your toes must be like arrows, your arms must be like iron. You have to think that if you kick, you try to kick the enemy dead. If you punch, you must thrust to kill. If you strike, then you strike to kill the enemy. This is the spirit you need in order to progress in your training."

~ Choshin Chibana

118

I don't think limits.

~ Usain Bolt

119

Where there is only a choice
between cowardice and violence, I
would advise violence.
  ~ Mohandas Gandhi

120

The best fighter is never angry.

~ Lao Tzu

121

The secret of change is to focus all
of your energy, not on fighting the
old, but building the new.

~ Socrates

122

I can think of no more worthwhile
aim than pursuing mastery in this
craft while transcending one's
own limitations.

~ Chris Matakas

123

Some Warriors look fierce, but are mild. Some seem timid, but are vicious. Look beyond appearances; position yourself for the advantage.

~ Deng Ming-Dao

124

Karate aims to build character, improve human behavior, and cultivate modesty; it does not, however, guarantee it.

~ Yasuhiro Konishi

125

All fixed set patterns are incapable
of adaptability or pliability. The
truth is outside of all fixed
patterns.
 ~ Bruce Lee

126

The will to win, the desire to
succeed, the urge to reach your
full potential... these are the keys
that will unlock the door to
personal excellence.
 ~ Confucius

127

Optimism is the faith that leads to achievement. Nothing can be done without hope and confidence.
~ Helen Keller

128

I have not failed 700 times, I have not failed once. I have succeeded in proving those 700 ways will not work. When I have eliminated the ways that will not work, I will find the way that will work.

~ Thomas Edison

129

Never give up, which is the lesson I learned from boxing. As soon as you learn to never give up, you have to learn the power and wisdom of unconditional surrender, and that one doesn't cancel out the other; they just exist as contradictions. The wisdom of it comes as you get older.

~ Kris Kristofferson

130

The 1st period is won by the best technician. The 2nd period is won by the kid in the best shape. The 3rd period is won by the kid with the biggest heart.

~ Dan Gable

131

Mental strength is really important because you either win or lose
in your mind. And I'm not solely
talking about sporting matches,
boxing events—anything you do,
you do it first with your mental
strength. And you can actually
train and develop it, and I am
responsible for what I'm saying
because I have experience with
that.

~ Wladimir Klitschko

132

Happiness is realizing your
dreams.

~ Mauricio "Shogun" Rua

133

I am a shark, the ground is my ocean, and most people don't know how to swim.

~ Jean Jacques Machado

134

It's less about the physical training. In the end, it is about the mental preparation. Boxing is a chess game. You have to be skilled enough and have trained hard enough to know how many different ways you can counter-attack in any situation, at any moment.

~ Jimmy Smits

135

Everybody's life has some
mythical quality. You struggle
against obstacles, you fight to get
to a higher level and there are
great loves.
 ~ Dolph Lundgren

136

Those who are skilled in combat
do not become angered, those who
are skilled at winning do not
become afraid. Thus the wise win
before the fight, while the ignorant
fight to win.
 ~ O Sensei Ueshiba

137

Pain is the best instructor, but no one wants to go to his class.

~ Hong Hi Choi

138

The important thing in strategy is to suppress the enemy's useful actions but allow his useless actions.

~ Miyamoto Musashi

139

A diamond with a flaw is worth
more than a pebble without
imperfections.
  ~ Chinese Proverb

140

The evolution of the sport is so
fast, if you slow down for a
second you are passed.

  ~ Chuck Lidell

141

Behind every champion is a team
that prepared him to become that
champion.
~ Anderson Silva

142

Failure will never overtake me if
my determination to succeed is
strong enough.
~ Og Mandino

143

It does not matter how slowly you
go as long as you do not stop.
 ~ Confucius

144

Gold medals aren't really made of
gold. They're made of sweat,
determination, and a hard-to-find
alloy called guts.
 ~ Dan Gable

145

You have to learn the rules of the game. And then you have to play better than anyone else.

~ Albert Einstein

146

Never be afraid to fail. Failure is only a stepping stone to improvement. Never be overconfident because that will block your improvement.

~ Tony Jaa

147

Gratitude unlocks the fullness of life. It turns what we have into enough, and more. It turns denial into acceptance, chaos to order, confusion to clarity. It can turn a meal into a feast, a house into a home, a stranger into a friend.
~ Melody Beattie

148

Doubt is removed by action. If you are not working, that's when doubt sets in.

~ Colin McGregor

149

All warfare is based on deception.
Hence, when able to attack, we
must seem unable; when using
our forces, we must seem inactive;
when we are near, we must make
the enemy believe we are far
away; when far away, we must
make him believe we are near.
Hold out baits to entice the
enemy. Feign disorder, and crush
him.

~ Sun Tzu

150

We are what we repeatedly do.
Excellence then, is not an act, but a
habit.

~ Aristotle

151

Don't hit at all if it is honorably possible to avoid hitting; but never hit softly.
 ~ Theodore Roosevelt

152

True courage is born only when it is accompanied by justice.
 ~ Masutatsu Oyama

153

What is a champion but a guy that didn't quit? Life is a continuous experience. You only fail by not learning.

~ Renzo Gracie

154

It's not the daily increase but daily decrease. Hack away at the unessential.

~ Bruce Lee

155
When life knocks you down,
slowly get back up, smile and say,
"you hit like a bitch."
 ~ Miguel Torres

156
I believe a lot in what I do and in
my work. I believe in me.

 ~ Lyoto Machida

157

A lot of us lead relatively sedentary lifestyles, so you have to motivate yourself and force yourself to go to the gym and do active things. The folks that have figured it out, found that thing that they love and made it a big part of their lives, it's easy for them to stay in shape.

~ Randy Couture

158

Bravery is being the only one who knows you're afraid.

~ Franklin P. Jones

159

Fall down seven times, get up eight.

~ Japanese Proverb

160

If I am going to do something, I do it 100% and I want to reach the top of the top. I want to be the top of the food chain. I am not happy to be number two.

~ Alexander Gustafsson

161

I'm a martial artist, and I don't train because I have a fight; I train because it's my lifestyle, and I'll train every day if I'm not hurt.
~ Georges St-Pierre

162

The one who has conquered himself is a far greater hero than he who has defeated a thousand times a thousand men.

~ Buddha

163
Goals achieved with little effort
are seldom worthwhile or lasting.
 ~ John Wooden

164
Fight adversity with passion.
 ~ Urijah Faber

165

I take inspiration from everyone
and everything. I am inspired by
current champions, former
champions, true competitors,
people dedicated to their dream,
hard workers, dreamers, believers,
achievers.
~ Colin McGregor

166

I'm just an ordinary man doing
extraordinary things.
~ BJ Penn

167

Your body will keep doing
whatever your mind tells it to do.
~ Pat Barry

168

Of old the expert in battle would
first make himself invincible and
then wait for his enemy to expose
his vulnerability.

~ Sun Tzu

169

Every tree and plant in the
meadow seemed to be dancing,
those which average eyes would
see as fixed and still.

~ Rumi

170

Teachers open the door, but you
must enter by yourself

~ Chinese Proverb

171

Given enough time, any man may master the physical. With enough knowledge, any man may become wise. It is the true warrior who can master both....and surpass the result.

~ Tien T'ai

172

A man who has attained mastery of an art reveals it in his every action.

~ Gogen Yamaguchi

173

If you always put limits on everything you do, physical or anything else, it will spread into your work and into your life. There are no limits. There are only plateaus, and you must not stay there, you must go beyond them.
~ Bruce Lee

174

Mental bearing (calmness), not skill, is the sign of a matured samurai. A Samurai therefore should neither be pompous nor arrogant.
~ Tsukahara Bokuden.

175

Remember… you are expressing
the technique, not doing the
technique.

~ Bruce Lee

176

Fighting is like life. You can show
and fail. That's no reason to quit.

~ Frank Mir

177

I think scars are like battle wounds
- beautiful, in a way. They show
what you've been through and
how strong you are for coming out
of it.

~ Demi Lovato

178

The past is a cancelled check, the
future is a promissory note and
today is all the cash you have.

~ Vitor Belfort

179

The primary objective of Jiu-Jitsu is to empower the weak who, for not having the physical attributes, are often intimidated. My Jiu-Jitsu is an art of self-defense in which rules and time limits are unacceptable. These are the reasons for which I can't support events that reflect an anti-Jiu-Jitsu.
  ~ Helio Gracie

180

Krav Maga heightens perception and transforms fear into something more productive.
  ~ Imi Lichtenfeld

Conclusion

For me, this book is an opportunity to give back to the martial arts community, as Krav Maga saved my life in many ways. While I have not been practicing martial arts my entire life, I have found that the principles from various disciplines have helped me to expand as a coach and practitioner of Krav Maga, not to mention as a man, father, leader, coach, businessman and more.

I believe that "wisdom not shared is wisdom wasted." There is such opportunity for us to grow and expand and help others do the same. This book is an attempt to reach out and motivate those I cannot work with directly due to geographical constraints. I still wanted to make an impact, so you can, in turn, make an impact on someone else.

Martial Arts and Krav Maga have taught me priceless lessons on emotional state regeneration, finding peace in the chaos, humility, slowing down time, increased quality of decision making while under stress, improved problem solving and so much more.

My hope is that you are able to use this collection as inspiration to help you get to the gym or help make someone else's life easier because you were able to give them a lift. This book, like the Bruce Lee quote above implies, is about helping us all grow and expand to the next level, whatever that is for us, in whatever shape or form it takes.

With the greatest respect for all martial artists, thank you.

"Be water, my friends."

~Dave

Transition and Reflection
By Walter Cardwell, 2nd Dan Black Belt, Tae Kwon Do
Owner of Alpha Krav Maga Richmond

As a kid, I first found football to be my sport of choice. Being a young strong male, I found that the sport allowed me to express myself and have fun while exuding great passion. At the time, unfortunately, my temperament did not allow me to be coached, and in many ways I got in my own way.

While I moved on to play semi-pro football and run track, it was only through studying martial arts—specifically Tae Kwon Do—which helped me to redirect my life and find a new, positive energy.

The excellent quotes that Dave Gerber has included in this book rekindled not only my motivation but also reminded me of a former self. One that, prior to martial arts, was negative and without focus. Like my own transition, Dave has done an amazing job of crossing over the different arts and providing people with a hands-on way to change their day, if not their life. Thank you for bringing this forward.

If you always put limits on everything you do, physical or anything else. It will spread into your work and into your life. There are no limits. There are only plateaus, and you must not stay there, you must go beyond them.

~Bruce Lee

Focus
By Dennis Amato, Alpha Krav Maga Black Belt
Owner of Alpha Krav Maga International gyms in Boston

I was someone who worked different jobs until ending up in the bar business, as I never really found my niche. When I stumbled my way into martial arts, I realized that to truly change and grow, my energies and priorities needed to be re-focused. I quit the bar business to turn my hobby into a career.

I credit Krav Maga as the inspiration for helping me change my life and actually save me from the negative influences that environment provided. A leap of faith, belief in myself and this ongoing journey have been the example I share with everyday people, like myself, who are looking to make real change.

We all need encouragement and support. This book provides the kind of inspiration everyone needs, regardless of which martial arts disciple they practice or what struggles they have or will overcome. I will keep this book and use it as a tool in my daily pursuit to help others expand upon their potential as well. Dave, very well put together!

Ever since I was a child, I have had this instinctive urge for expansion and growth. To me, the function and duty of a quality human being is the sincere and honest development of one's potential.
~Bruce Lee

Afterword

By John Tiano, 6th Dan Black Belt, Owner RockStar
Martial Arts, Stoughton, Massachusetts

In many gyms, bars, family rooms, garages, home gyms, man caves, rec centers and other places, guys (and women) battle it out in arguments about which form of martial arts is the best.

Everyone is going to select their main style based upon their experience and exposure growing up, whether on television or training from childhood. The reality is they all have their purpose. They are all good for what they are meant to deliver on. Nothing more, nothing less. This is why it is important to train many styles. In order to appreciate and value the style you focus on, learning more about the overall martial arts contexts, the movements of styles not practiced by the mainstream. This is what it is all about!

The great thing about this book is that Dave clearly meant to cross over the unseen boundaries and politics of the different martial arts communities to bring us a collection of thoughts and wisdom that everyone can benefit from. This book is a bridge that interconnects so many of the different disciplines being trained throughout the world. Reality is, those who practice martial arts get tired, hit plateaus, have to overcome injuries or just the lack of desire on any given day to train. This book of quotes will help jumpstart any person or teacher looking to make a difference in their own training, the support of other professional and every day martial artists. It is something that I will keep close by and refer to when creating lessons and seminars, not to mention when motivating myself and my staff.

About the Special Contributor
Bob Zacharias

 Bob Zacharias started training in Taekwondo and Judo in 1986. He later entered the U.S. Army and was stationed at Fort Bragg, N.C. MOS (91A). He was a Combat Medic for 27th Engineer Battalion (C) (A). and Trained members of the 27th Engineer Battalion (C) (A) in practical application of hand to hand combat. He conducted training on an ongoing basis in practical self defense for selected members of CAG.

Bob worked for the Jacksonville, Florida Sheriff's Office as a part of the internal security for the Duval County Courthouse in Jacksonville. He earned first degree Taekwondo.black belt in 1981 and later began full contact kick boxing. He began instructing Taekwondo and practical self-defense for Bill Clark's Karate Academy in Jacksonville.

Bob was boxing partner for Clay Davis—title holder for the 1983 South Eastern Lightweight Champion. He became a certified instructor for the American Taekwondo Association. In 1983, he earned Second Degree Black Belt in Taekwondo. He was a team member for the AmericanTaekwondo Association with the job of incorporating practical self defense into the organization's curriculum. Bob was recalled to Active Duty for Desert Shield and Desert Storm with the FloridaNational Guard, in 1991.

In 1992 Bob earned Third Degree Black Belt in Taekwondo, and Seventh Degree Black Belt in Taekwondo in 2011. At this time, he started training in Krav Maga under the Chief Instructor and founder of Alpha Krav MagaInternational, Sam Sade. He was appointed as Board Member to Alpha Krav Maga Internationaland created and implemented the Active Shooter First Responder Course within ZUMAS MartialArts Academy.

Bob was Chief Martial Arts Instructor for the Jacksonville Karate Academy that implemented training for single stick, double stick, knife, bo-staff, kickboxing, and ground fighting techniques for certified instructors and trainee instructors. He opened ZUMAS Martial Arts Academy in Williamsburg, Virginia in 1994.

Bob was ranked in the top competitors worldwide list for the American Taekwondo Association and Song Ahm Taekwondo Federation, in the Lightweight Division. He ranked in the top competitors worldwide list for the American Taekwondo Association and Song Ahm Taekwondo Federation, in the Lightweight Division.

He is a Phase C Instructor Certified with Alpha Krav 2014 Maga International. Implemented Defensive Tactics System (DTS) within ZUMAS Martial Arts Academy.

About the Author

Dave Gerber is President and founder of Synergy Development & Training, LLC. This innovative organizational solutions company specializes in helping businesses, government agencies, organizations, schools and individuals build leadership capacity, *use conflict* as an opportunity to increase performance and revenue, and reduce risk.

Dave helps individuals understand the impact of conflict and specializes in motivating others to increase and actualize their potential, regardless of industry as he has worked within many. He has worked with business owners, executives, managers, employees of all kinds, CEOs, military officers, the space and intelligence community, business development directors, doctors, lawyers, engineers, educators and more in a coaching, training, speaking and consulting capacity. He has hands-on experience working with over 10,000 training participants and students of all ages, races, backgrounds and ability levels.

Dave received a Bachelor's Degree in Sociology from Ithaca College in New York and a Master's Degree in Education from St. Joseph's University in Philadelphia. He also holds a Senior Executive Leadership certificate and a Leadership Coaching (ICF) certificate from Georgetown University in Washington, D.C. He holds Executive Certificates in Negotiations, Leadership and Management from Notre Dame. He has multiple certificates in Workplace Conflict Processes, Workplace Mediation and Conflict Resolution, Commercial, Federal Workplace and Family

Mediation from the Northern Virginia Mediation Service at George Mason. Dave brings over 20 years of varied conflict management, teaching, coaching and educator training experience as well. He has also written several books with more out shortly.

Lastly, Dave is a certified Krav Maga Instructor and Self-Defense coach. He is the affiliate owner and head coach of Alpha Krav Maga International (AKMI) Northern Virginia/DC Metro. Additionally, Dave is the AKMI Leadership Program Director. His desire to serve, support and lead leaders is limitless.

Consistently throughout his life and ongoing legacy, Dave, with great zeal, has attempted to improve the lives of others at nearly all costs.

For More Information

www.synergy-selfdefense.com

About Dave:

www.synergydt.com

www.Davegerber.info

About This Book:

www.onfireleadershipquotes.com

More Testimonials from Martial Artists

"As a martial arts instructor, I can say this is a must have! Reading these quotes reminded me of the great journey I have taken and am still on. I will use this to support my students and others as they take their own path."

~ Byron Ferguson, Martial Arts Instructor
  3rd Dan Black Belt

"It is quotes like these that continually feed a martial artist's desire to learn, grow and get the best out of life, both on and off the mat!"

~ Don Cho, Martial Arts Instructor, 1st Dan Black Belt
  Marine Corps Reservist

"This is an inspiring collection of quotes. The men, women, children, and instructors who practice martial arts as a way of life can use this at any time along their journey. Anyone who reads this will want to read it again!"

~ Mark McIntyre, Martial Arts Instructor, Carpenter

"This book of martial arts quotes has everything—inspiration, motivation, historical presence and great energy! Whether you practice martial arts or have a friend or family member that needs a boost, this will re-ignite the fire! I look at it daily!"

~ Bill Jackson
  Martial Artist, multiple disciplines, US Army (retired)

www.synergy-selfdefense.com

Notes